SUFFERING & COMFORT IN CHRIST

A STUDY OF 2 CORINTHIANS

GARY C. HAMPTON

ISBN-10: 0615770142
ISBN-13: 978-0615770147

Published by Start2Finish Books
PO Box 660675 #54705
Dallas, TX 75266-0675
www.start2finish.org

Printed in the United States of America

Cover Design: Josh Feit, Evangela.com

CONTENTS

1. The God of All Comfort   5

2. Forgiveness: Discipline's Desired End   12

3. Thew New Covenant   16

4. Seeing the Unseen   20

5. Being Reconciled to God   24

6. Paul's Ministry & the Desired Response   29

7. A Message from Their Father in the Faith   33

8. Completing a Commitment   37

9. Giving   42

10. The Spiritual War & Paul's Authority   46

11. Paul's Apostleship & Suffering   51

12. A Vision, a Thorn, & Love   57

13. Paul's Trip and Closing Thoughts   62

1

THE GOD OF ALL COMFORT

2 CORINTIANS 1:1-24

The second letter to the church at Corinth was apparently written not long after the first. We will observe the facts surrounding it as Paul writes. Suffice it to say, most of the church at Corinth had taken the first letter well and were striving to do as it instructed. However, a strong, vocal minority was still stirring up trouble and leveling an attack against Paul.

GREETINGS

The opening verse, combined with 10:1, gives solid internal evidence for the authorship of Paul. The apostle started answering his accusers immediately, stressing that he was an apostle chosen by God, not men. He placed Timothy's name with his in the introduction, perhaps because he had helped establish the church in Corinth (Acts 18:1, 5) and had been sent to correct problems there (1 Cor. 4:17). This letter was addressed to "the whole of Achaia," which would include Athens in the Roman province. The first letter seems to have been limited to the smaller Greek sense of "Achaia," which would not have included Athens. This is thought because 1 Cor. 16:15 calls Stephanas the "firstfruits," however the inclusion of Athens would make one of those baptized after the Mars Hill discourse firstfruits (2 Cor. 1:1; Acts 17:34).

Paul prayed that the Corinthian church might have grace and peace from God the Father and Jesus Christ his Son. It is interesting how the apostle adopted both the Greek and Hebrew terms of greeting. The combination certainly makes for an appropriate prayer for God's people in all ages (2 Cor. 1:2).

THE GOD OF ALL COMFORT

Paul went on to thank God and honor him as the source of mercy and comfort (2 Cor. 1:3-4). The singer of Israel sang of God in Psa. 86:15—"But You, O Lord, are a God full of compassion, and gracious, Longsuffering and abundant in mercy and truth." As McGarvey and Pendleton wrote, "Paul regarded affliction as a school wherein one who is comforted of God is thereby instructed and fitted to become a dispenser of comfort unto others" (170). Comfort, according to G. Campbell Morgan, "literally means strengthened, sustained....This is more than consolation, it is underpinning. It is coming to the side of someone and disannulling all his loneliness and his difficulty—comfort" (227).

Jesus suffered persecution and ridicule, just as his followers (Christians) will suffer when they try to imitate Christ. Peter said, "But rejoice to the extent that you partake of Christ's sufferings, that when His glory is revealed, you may also be glad with exceeding joy" (1 Pet. 4:13). That joy should arise from knowing the promise that all will "work together for good to those who love God" (Rom. 8:28). Also, if a Christian suffers, he will be greatly rewarded (2 Cor. 1:5; 4:17, 2 Tim. 2:12).

Paul endured persecution so others might hear the gospel message and be converted by his willingness to suffer to proclaim it. The comfort Paul received served to comfort those who also suffered since they knew God would aid them. Those who stood with Paul and the true gospel would likely face the same hardships Paul faced. However, the apostle knew that all would come out for their good since God would give them the same comfort he had received (2 Cor. 1:6-7).

GOD DELIVERED PAUL

During Paul's trip to Ephesus, trouble arose between the apostle and the devoted followers of Diana, who were led by Demetrius (Acts 19:23-20:1). There is no doubt he saw great opportunities to further the gospel of Christ (1 Cor. 16:8-9). However, he told the Corinthian brethren that he feared for his life. Acts 20:1 pictures him as disturbed enough to leave Ephesus suddenly. It seems Paul's escape was so narrow that he assumed he would die. He gave up on his own power to escape and placed complete reliance on God. He was greatly comforted by knowing that God can raise the dead (2 Cor. 1:8-9).

Paul knew God had delivered him, and believed He would continue to do so until his purpose was accomplished. Such great evidence of God's power caused Paul to trust God to deliver him from all enemies. The Corinthians had helped Paul during times of trial by praying for him. Paul's deliverance was granted, in part, by the prayers of many brethren. So Paul says all should pray to God specifically thanking Him for that deliverance (2 Cor. 1:10-11).

PAUL'S SINCERITY

If his words sounded boastful, Paul's conscience could withstand the test of God's scrutiny and still show him holy and truthful.

He had not lived as one after earthly gain, but as one following God's instruction. This was true in all his actions and especially in Corinth. His dealings with the Corinthians could withstand the inspection of the divisive teachers (2 Cor. 1:12).

Paul had used the same sincere approach in his writings to them. He had written plainly and without double meaning. All his writings were public, open to anyone's inspection. He did not write privately to some to clarify or change his meaning. He hoped they would continue to confess the truth of his words until the day they died. If they continued to acknowledge his truthful words till death, they could glory in one another in judgment. Paul could be proud of them as his children in the faith, and they could be proud of him as their father in the faith (2 Cor. 1:13-14).

A CHANGE IN PLANS

Since they had mutual pride and respect for one another, Paul had confidently planned to visit them on the way to and from Macedonia, but had changed plans to give them time to correct the problems he addressed in the first letter. If they made the corrections, their visit would obviously be better. Too, God had blessed him with a great opportunity in Ephesus (1 Cor. 16:5-9; Acts 19:1-40). They were important to him, so he changed his plans from two short visits to one longer one so they might receive extra teaching and strength. He thought so highly of the Corinthian brethren that he wanted them to see him off on his journey to take money to the needy saints in Judea (2 Cor. 1:15-16).

Paul asked the Corinthians if he acted like an unscrupulous person of this world who would promise one thing and do another with light regard for his honor. The apostle went on to tell them that he was just like the God he had preached to them. God was good to his word, and so his servant Paul was true to his word. He, unlike the false teachers or a modern day crooked politician, would not affirm and deny the same statement (2 Cor. 1:17-18).

Silas, Timothy, and Paul had all preached and worked together during the apostle's first visit in Corinth (Acts 18:5). They had, on that first visit, preached a Christ who kept his promises. No matter how many promises God makes, he will keep them all. God also sent Jesus to be the "Amen," or "so be it," to all of God's promises (2 Cor. 1:19-20).

GOD'S VERIFICATION OF PAUL'S SINCERITY

God had established Paul's sincerity by backing him with signs and miracles. Since God was a promise keeper, He would not support one who was dishonest. God had anointed Paul as an apostle and placed His seal on him to show His ownership. The Holy Spirit working through Paul was like God putting up enough money to guarantee payment of His part of the bargain. The Spirit was evidence that Paul was working in God's behalf (2 Cor. 1:21-22).

Paul called God as a witness since God knows all things and can search man's heart. He wanted them to know that he did not come to Corinth because he wanted to spare them added hardships. The apostle could not rule over their faith. Instead, he revealed the will of God to them in the hope that they would grow in faith. He wanted his time with them to be happy, which it would be if they stood firm in God's truth. Paul refused to come to them while they needed discipline for their weakness in the faith.

REFLECTION & DISCUSSION

1. Describe Paul's opening words to the church of God in Corinth.

2. What are the blessings found in serving the "God of all comfort"?

3. How does Jesus' life relate to our times of suffering?

4. How might times of distress, like Paul endured, be used by Christians to aid others going through times of distress?

5. How was Paul able to go through so many difficult times?

6. What lessons can be learned by the fact that Paul kept all of his communication open to anyone's inspection?

7. Why had Paul not visited the church in Corinth at the time he had originally planned?

8. Describe some times when it might be good to give someone more time before paying them a visit.

9. How did God, Christ, and Paul value their promises?

2

FORGIVENESS: DISCIPLINE'S DESIRABLE END

2 CORINTHIANS 2:1-17

SORROW

Paul had made them sorry by the discipline of the earlier letter and was hoping to be made happy by their changed lives. His love for the church and desire to see them grow in faith made it well worth the wait before coming. Only those he had caused to be sorry could make him happy. Their standing firm in the faith would bring rejoicing (2 Cor. 2:1-2).

Paul wrote his first letter to the church in Corinth to get them to change. Specifically, he was concerned that they were tolerating sin. He directed them to withdraw from the disorderly brother to save his soul. He warned them to change and confidently believed they would make him rejoice. He had not rejoiced in the evil that was present in the church, but was brought to a state of anguish (1 Cor. 4:21; 5:1). He demonstrated his love for them by correcting and disciplining them (2 Cor. 2:3-4).

The fornicator Paul mentioned in 1 Cor. 5 had brought sorrow to Paul through his sinful acts. Paul saw his sorrow in the matter as nothing compared to the sorrow of the church. The apostle had encouraged them to withdraw fellowship from him to bring him to repentance. They seem to have been successful in their actions, and Paul pleaded with them to forgive the penitent man and accept him back, lest his sorrow and shame drive him to Satan for lack of hope. Just as Paul had instructed them to discipline the fornicator, he wanted them to forgive him and publicly display their love for him (2 Cor. 2:5-8).

Paul had used this case of fellowship as a test of their willingness to obey. They had proven faithful. He was in agreement with any action taken under God's direction. In fact, he indicated that any action that is taken in accord with Christ's law is actually taken in conjunction with the Lord. The purpose of discipline is to save the sinner (1 Cor. 5:3-5). In a similar manner, the apostle urged the church to forgive in order to defeat Satan. If we are unmerciful or unforgiving, Satan can use that to harden the penitent sinner completely against the truth (2 Cor. 2:9-11).

TRIUMPHANT IN CHRIST

The apostle's concern for the brethren in Corinth made it difficult for him to seize the door of opportunity the Lord opened in Troas. His troubled wait was cut short when he received no word from Titus and moved on to Macedonia. His anxiety over the Corinthian response to the first letter thus hindered his preaching (2 Cor. 2:12-13).

Paul was thankful for the good word that Titus brought from Corinth. He also thanked God for the continual triumphs he experienced so long as he remained in Christ. G. Campbell Morgan saw this as a picture of a Roman triumph (235). The knowledge of Christ is like an incense burned by the victor and carried as he goes. The apostle to the Gentiles, in a similar way, saw Christ's messengers as producing an aroma. To those who accepted the gospel, they gave off the sweet smell of victory. To those who rejected the good news, they were like the incense the Roman captives smelled when going to their death (2 Cor. 2:14-15).

Those who reject God's plan to save man face death, while the believers look forward to life eternal. Paul asked who was prepared to deliver such a great message. Unfortunately, he knew there were many who would corrupt God's word, changing it to suit popular demands and their own selfish desires. The word "peddling" originally was used of a tavern keeper who would shortchange his customers and dilute supposedly pure drinks. Paul intended to deliver a pure gospel, remembering God could see all. He was also constantly aware that he was one of Christ's spokesmen (2 Cor. 2:16-17).

REFLECTION & DISCUSSION

1. How did Paul's desire for a good visit motivate him to change plans?

2. How did Paul demonstrate his love for the Corinthian church?

3. Describe the action Paul now urged the church to take in regards to the penitent. Why was this necessary?

4. How can forgiveness, or the lack of it, either advance or stall the attack of Satan?

5. Discuss things you glean from Bible dictionaries and encyclopedias about the Roman victory march.

6. What did Paul intend to do with the gospel? How did he think others would treat it?

3

THE NEW COVENANT

2 CORINTHIANS 3

PAUL'S LETTER OF RECOMMENDATION

It seems Paul was criticized for using personal examples in his first epistle, as nine uses of the word "commend" would indicate (3:1; 4:2; 5:12; 6:4; 7:11; 10:12, 18 (twice); 12:11). The apostle makes it clear that he needs neither boasting nor letters of commendation as the Lord's apostle. In fact, he said they were his letter. Their conversion was deeply etched in his heart and was on display in Corinth, a center of world trade. Christ was the author, Paul, his secretary, the heart the place of record, and the Holy Spirit the means of leaving a lasting impression (2 Cor. 3:1-3; Jer. 31:31-34; 1 Thess. 1:8; Rom. 1:8).

Assured by Christ, Paul confidently counted them as his letter of recommendation. Of course, the work he did in Corinth was through God's power (1 Cor. 15:10). God made Paul a messenger, not of legal age, but of a spiritual age. This new law gives life in place of condemnation (2 Cor. 3:4-6; Rom. 8:1-4).

THE GREATER GLORY OF THE NEW COVENANT

The law of Moses was written in stone, even though it was transitory (Gal. 3:21-25). That law condemned men to die since they were not perfect. Yet Moses, as a minister of that covenant, was glorified to the point that no one could look upon his face. Moses' law was directed to the outward man and condemned, yet brought glory. The law brought by the Spirit and directed to the inward man should bring more glory (2 Cor. 3:7-8). Christ promised to send the Holy Spirit, describing his purpose by saying, "He will glorify Me, for He will take of what is Mine and declare it to you" (John 16:7, 14). Thus, Paul described him as the "Spirit of Christ" (Rom. 8:9).

The Old Law could not free man from sin while the New can. Since the Old brought glory, the New should outshine it as the sun outshines the moon. Even though the Old Law was made glorious, the New, in comparison, made it as if it had no glory. Like the rising sun obscures the moon, the New Law obscures the Old. It remains while the other is obscured, thus displaying its greater glory (2 Cor. 3:9-11).

Because we have hope of life and not of condemnation, Paul was not timid in speech. Knowing God was on his side, he spoke openly (2 Cor. 3:12).

SEEING CHRIST'S GLORY WITH THE VEIL REMOVED

Just as Moses used a veil to cover the glory shining on his face (Exod. 34:33), so he used types and shadows to cover the glory of the Lord. Christians can now see Christ's glory with the veil of types and shadows taken away. In reading Moses' Law, the veil of types and shadows still covered Christ for the Jews. Their hardened hearts refused to see Christ. However, they could see him in the New Testament (2 Cor. 3:13-14).

Those rejecting Christ still fail to see him in the Old Testament. They overlook the purpose of that covenant (Gal. 3:24). However, those who sincerely strove to see God's will found the veil removed. Earlier (vv. 6-7), Moses was used to stand for the letter, while Christ, in the same way, stands for the Spirit. Freedom is found in Christ, particularly by seeing him clearly. Christians see his glory reflected in the new covenant, and their faces are made to shine with his glory much as Moses' face shone after he had been with God (2 Cor. 3:15-18). This transformation comes about through immersing oneself in God's Word and renewing the mind (Psa. 1:1-2; 2 Tim. 2:15; Rom. 12:1-2). The glory of God will be thereby seen in a Christian's earthly life while he waits for the glory to come (1 John 3:2).

REFLECTION & DISCUSSION

1. How are a teacher's students considered to be letters of recommendation?

2. Discuss the contrasting glory produced by Moses' law and that brought by the Spirit.

3. What kept Paul from being timid in his speech?

4. What "veil" covered the face of Christ under Moses' law?

5. What makes the faces of Christians shine with Christ's glory?

4

SEEING THE UNSEEN

2 CORINTHIANS 4

PAUL & THE FALSE TEACHERS

In 2 Cor. 3:6, Paul had said he was a minister of the new covenant. The apostle, with full knowledge that he had tried to destroy Christianity, was ever thankful for God's mercy, which allowed him to preach the gospel (1 Tim. 1:12-13). That mercy and great message gave him courage to endure persecution (2 Cor. 4:1).

Apparently, the false teachers Paul opposed had done things in secret which they would have been ashamed to have exposed. It also appears that they would use any means at their disposal to gain followers. They may even have misused God's Word to escape exposure and punishment. Paul didn't use the false teachers' approach. Instead, he openly proclaimed the truth (Acts 20:26-27) with the realization that he would be tested by men in God's sight (2 Cor. 4:2).

Even though Paul proclaimed the truth openly, there were those who did not see that truth. As 3:14 would show, there were some who could not see the truth because they did not want to. These were "those who are perishing" by choice. Sinful man made Satan his god, thus giving him control over the world. To retain his power, Satan has to blind his subjects so they cannot see the light of the truth (2 Cor. 4:3-4; Luke 8:12).

It may be that the false teachers proclaimed themselves, but Paul saw himself as a servant for Jesus' sake. He only reflected the glory of the Savior. To proclaim Jesus as Lord is to tell others that He is Master, Ruler, and Savior. Those who knew the Word of God should have remembered that He gave light to a newly created world (Gen. 1:3). In much the same way, the Father sent Jesus to be the Light of the world (Isa. 60:1-2; John 1:1-5). Jesus reflected God's light and gave man knowledge of God that he might give to others (2 Cor. 4:5-6).

GOD'S PROCLAIMERS WILL OVERCOME

The treasure would be the gospel. That treasure is carried to the world in earthly vessels—that is, our bodies. Because the body is weak, the greatness of the message it carries is better seen. Also, it is easy to see such a frail body is not the source of such a powerful message (2 Cor. 4:7).

Paul also pictured gospel proclaimers as soldiers fighting for the gospel treasure. He knew the enemy might move in on all sides at close quarters. The apostle, however, said that God's soldier would still have room to wield his sword and defend himself with his shield. Though he might be greatly troubled by the close fighting, he should not lose hope. In the thick of the battle, the soldier might seek safety by running. Even then, Paul said God would not leave him in a helpless state. In fact, the apostle said God would not allow His soldier to be defeated even if he was overtaken by the enemy and knocked down (2 Cor. 4:8-9).

Paul and other proclaimers of the good news suffered persecution like Jesus and died, as it were, because of it (1 Cor. 15:31; Rom.

8:36; Phil. 3:10; Col. 1:24; Gal. 6:17). Paul's sufferings caused the self-ish man to be dead and Christ to be seen in the apostle's response to that suffering (Gal. 2:20). That death, brought about by suffering for Christ, also brings eternal life through the gospel, especially for those who hear us proclaim despite trials. Despite affliction, which might have caused Paul to give up, he took the attitude of the psalm-ist who was compelled to speak because he believed in God (2 Cor. 4:10-13; Psa. 116:10).

The ultimate source of the proclaimers' belief and hope rested in the resurrection. It was the knowledge that all believers, including the bearer of good news, would one day overcome the grave and be taken home to be with the Lord that kept them strong and faithful. Everything done in the service of the gospel is done for the believer. They were taught that they might receive God's grace and, in turn, that grace received by them might glorify God (2 Cor. 4:14-15).

A PROPER VIEW OF SUFFERING

Paul confidently believed death would be followed by a resur-rection. He knew his suffering brought glory to God, thus he would not give up hope and quit fighting. The apostle's physical body was gradually being destroyed by suffering. The spiritual man, in con-trast, daily grew stronger because of the same suffering. The apos-tle counted his troubles as light because of the reward withstanding them would bring. Trials are temporary, while the reward will be eternal. Scripture clearly teaches that bearing up under tribulation will bring reward (2 Cor. 4:16-17; 2 Tim. 2:12; 1 Pet. 4:13; Rom. 8:17).

Jesus left us the example that we should respond to worldly trouble by obeying God (Phil. 2:7-11). If we think only in terms of this world, we may not be able to bear suffering. The Christian thinks in terms of eternity and the spiritual rewards to come (2 Cor. 4:18; Col. 3:1-4).

REFLECTION & DISCUSSION

1. Discuss the nature of the approach used by the false teachers in Corinth.

2. What was Paul's approach to preaching in Corinth?

3. What illustrations did Paul use for those proclaiming the gospel and the message itself?

4. What is the foundation of the hope held by gospel proclaimers?

5. How might Paul's view of suffering change our attitudes towards our own suffering?

5

BEING RECONCILED TO GOD

THE SPIRIT'S NEW HOME

Being from a Jewish background may have caused Paul to refer to man's current, physical body as a tabernacle, while referring to the future spiritual body as a house or dwelling place. After all, the glory of God dwelt in a tent while the temple was being built. By inspiration, Paul knew that if the fleshly body were destroyed, a spiritual body would replace it. The spirit would separate from the body at death and the body return to dust. The new body would be specially suited for life in heaven (2 Cor. 5:1; Jas 2:26; Eccles. 12:7). Peter used comparable language in 2 Pet. 1:13-14 when he wrote, "Yes, I think it is right, as long as I am in this tent, to stir you up by reminding you, knowing that shortly I must put off my tent, just as our Lord Jesus Christ showed me."

While one is enduring life's suffering, it is natural to long for that better specially-prepared house (or clothing). The apostle longed for the day of the Lord's coming when he might lay aside his physical body and put on the spiritual. Paul did not long for death because it brought separation of soul and body (or nakedness). Rather, he was willing to face death because of the new body awaiting him on the other side (2 Cor. 5:2-4).

God told about the immortal body which awaits the Christian and how to reach it. He gave the Holy Spirit as a pledge that He would keep the promise of a new body. Paul told the Ephesian church of many of the things Christians have in Christ. "In Him you also trusted, after you heard the word of truth, the gospel of your salvation; in whom also, having believed, you were sealed with the Holy Spirit of promise, who is the guarantee of our inheritance until the redemption of the purchased possession, to the praise of His glory" (1:13-14). Paul knew, because of such assurance, that this earthly home was not to be preferred to death, through which Christians can be at home with the Lord (2 Cor. 5:5-6).

Faith is the assurance each Christian has of a new body in the heavens. While it cannot be seen, its coming existence is known because of faith (Heb. 11:1). No wonder the apostle could desire death! He had no need to fear because death would allow him to be with the Lord (2 Cor. 5:7-8).

PAUL'S DESIRE & DEVOTION

The Corinthians' father in the faith did not grow lazy, even though he had assurance. Instead, he wanted to please God, whether it be in his physical body, absent from the Lord, or with the Lord (at home). Therefore, he could not afford to let down his guard, knowing all deeds will be laid open before Christ's judgment seat. Each will be rewarded on the basis of those deeds, so Paul took aim toward heaven to avoid missing being at home with the Lord. Fearing the Lord because of His power to judge all deeds, Paul sought to please him by persuading men. God would know his right intentions since

He saw all, and Paul hoped the Corinthians could now also see his good intentions and actions (2 Cor. 5:9-11).

The apostle was striving to give the brethren in Corinth enough knowledge to compare his actions with those of the teachers opposing him. He did not need, or intend, to boast. Those opposing him were fond of putting on an outward show, like presenting letters of recommendation. Paul had spiritual facts to thoroughly recommend him. His opponents said that he was mad, but all the actions they described as madness were directed in God's service. Actions taken by the apostle that would be viewed as sane were also aimed at strengthening the church. He simply could not be successfully accused of building up himself (2 Cor. 5:12-13).

Paul was devoted in his service to Christ, who would have him serve man. Though the apostle might have been tempted to neglect this service, the love of Christ caused him to continue in it. He especially felt compelled to serve since Christ had representatively died for all. Paul was thus dead to sin and self, and alive in Christ (Rom. 6:1-11; Gal. 2:20; Col. 3:3). Christians should ever live for their Lord since he died for them (2 Cor. 5:14-15; Rom. 12:1-2).

CHANGES BROUGHT ABOUT IN BAPTISM

Paul did not judge men in light of worldly thinking once he had been converted and become a part of the spiritual body of Christ. This was true, even though Paul had judged Christ by that standard before his conversion. This thought should have been particularly powerful to the apostle's Jewish readers who put so much stock in genealogies. Christians are spiritual and should be judged by spiritual standards. They should not be rejected because they are Gentiles or accepted because they are Jews. Fleshly desires are laid aside at baptism and a new life begun (2 Cor. 5:16-17).

The new man in Christ lives a life completely planned and re-vealed by God, who sent Christ to die that we might be made friends again with him. God gave us a means of having our sins forgotten and re-establishing our friendship with him. In turn, he wants us to tell others the terms of becoming God's friends (2 Cor. 5:18-19).

An ambassador carries messages from the king to others. Paul carried the message of salvation to the world, because Christ's blood had cleansed him of sin. As Christ's messenger, he pleaded with men to become God's friend through the washing away of sin. The strength of Paul's plea lay in the fact that God loved us enough to send a sinless Son to die for sinful man (2 Cor. 5:20-21).

REFLECTION & DISCUSSION

1. How might Paul's view of the physical body impact a Christian's thinking?

2. Give some reasons for the Christian's hope of heaven and a new body.

3. How can Christians have the same ultimate objective in life that Paul had?

4. Discuss the reason(s) Paul felt compelled to serve Christ and man.

5. What type of life should be lived by the new man in Christ?

6

PAUL'S MINISTRY &
THE DESIRED RESPONSE

2 CORINTHIANS 6:1-7:1

A DESCRIPTION OF PAUL'S MINISTRY

As he said at the close of the previous chapter, Paul considered himself to be an ambassador for Christ, especially as he worked with the Lord to save the Corinthians. Paul pleaded with them to remain faithful so they would not be turned away from the gospel. He then quoted Isa. 49:8 to prove God's continual interest in man's salvation. God is always ready to receive sinful man, but man is limited to the present since it will never happen again and the future is not assured. The apostle to the Gentiles lived his life in such a way that it would not hinder his preaching and thereby cause men to refuse his appeal to accept God's plan of salvation (2 Cor. 6:1-3).

His life stood as a witness and letter of recommendation. Instead of hindering those who might believe, it showed how completely he believed what he said. Paul had suffered quietly, knowing that a day of reward would come (Matt. 10:22). "Afflictions" may be the general persecution of the church with "necessities" being the want caused by these. "Distresses" would convey the idea of times when one is pushed into a corner out of which no human help can get him. Five times Paul received "stripes" from Jewish whips and three times from Roman rods (2 Cor. 11:24-25). Luke, in Acts 16:24, told Theophilus that the apostle was imprisoned, which may be the occasion referred to here. Paul was in "tumults" or "tossed to and fro," so often that there is no need to mention all of them. "Labors" would be working with his hands. On other occasions, he watched and labored with the brethren all night. He even missed meals in devotion to his work (2 Cor. 6:4-5).

Despite all that he had gone through, Paul had remained holy, not allowing trials to cause him to compromise the truth. He quietly suffered all the trials and was kind to his greatest tormentors. The Holy Spirit gave Paul strength, and he rose to a true love of Christ and his service. The apostle relied on God's word and power. He was ready to defend with God's righteous armor on the left hand and attack with God's righteousness on the right. He had been honored by converts and dishonored by Jews and Judaizers. Each side gave a different account of him, with some thinking of him as a fraud, but God knew he was a faithful servant. While his enemies refused to recognize him, God's people knew him well. Some tried to kill him, but God saved him. He had to suffer, yet not more than he could bear. This life was sorrowful for Paul, but he expected to rejoice in the next life. He had no money, but he gave others God's Word. He gave up all here, yet expected rich reward in the hereafter (2 Cor. 6:6-10).

THE RESPONSE OF THE CORINTHIAN CHURCH

In Paul's first letter to the Corinthian brethren, the troubles at Corinth had caused him to have a heart narrowed with concern for them. He also had been careful to keep his lips close together because of his determination to say the right things. As he wrote the second letter, the apostle found his heart expanded and his lips freed by the basically good response to his earlier appeals. If there was any guarded approach to their relationship at the time of this writing, it was on their part, not his. He longed for them to open up to his love (2 Cor. 6:11-13).

Paul appealed to the Corinthian Christians not to form relationships with unbelievers that would hinder their service to God. So long as it was possible to have peaceful relationships with unbelievers that would not affect their service to God adversely, they could continue (1 Cor. 5:9-10; 7:12-13). Those who would force Christians into a mold of wickedness were, under Paul's directions, to be shunned. He specifically mentioned "Belial," which means "worthless fellow," a likely reference to Satan (2 Cor. 6:14-15).

The apostle likened Christians to buildings, or temples, consecrated to the service of God. In what appears to be a loose quotation from Ezek. 37:26-27, Paul indicated that God dwells in those who are true believers, those who control their actions guided by the will of God (John 14:23). It is unthinkable to allow the wicked to have an evil influence on the inward man that houses God. In another quote, from Isa. 52:11, the apostle demonstrated that God's people must not allow wickedness to be within them. Next, he quoted from Hos. 1:10 and Isa. 43:6 to show that those who do purify the inward man will be adopted as God's children. God's followers can allow the wicked to influence them to evil only if they spurn this loving promise of adoption into God's great family. Those who realized the blessings associated with the promised adoption were enjoined to cleanse the inward man so that they would be pure for God's entrance. All who would be a part of the Almighty's family should fear his wrath if he should find a dirty dwelling place (2 Cor. 6:16-7:1).

REFLECTION & DISCUSSION

1. Why must sinful men obey *today*?

2. Use the book of Acts to discover times Paul went through various difficulties.

3. Discuss some of the contrasts found in Paul's life.

4. What value can be found in quiet consideration before responding to the actions or questions of others?

5. Why is it important to avoid wickedness and grow in purity?

7

A MESSAGE FROM THEIR FATHER IN THE FAITH

2 CORINTHIANS 7:2-16

A PLEA FOR THEM TO MAKE ROOM IN THEIR HEARTS

Paul, who was their father in the faith, appealed to the Corinthian Christians to make room for him in their hearts. They had no reason to be closed against him, since he had not led any man into sin, corrupted any man's morals or faith, or defrauded anyone out of their money. The apostle did not say these things to condemn them as if they were ungrateful or falsely accusing him. He would have liked to have lived and died with them, even as he had told them before (2 Cor. 7:2-3).

Paul's love for them was so great that it allowed him to speak openly with them about problems. He also told others of their good deeds and was glad to suffer in their behalf. So great was his concern for them that he could not rest until he heard from them, which reminds us of what he had already said in 2 Cor. 2:12-13. The apostle faced outward trials while inwardly worrying about the Corinthian reaction to his earlier letter (2 Cor. 7:4-5).

COMFORTING WORDS FROM TITUS

God comforts the downtrodden, so it should be no surprise that he comforted Paul with the appearance of Titus. Paul's Gentile son in the faith brought a good report from Corinth and demonstrated that he was positively impacted by their response. Titus must have been visibly satisfied with the results. He told of the Corinthian sorrow at having grieved Paul, as well as their desire, or longing, to see Paul. He likewise told the apostle of the way they had enthusiastically carried out his instructions (2 Cor. 7:6-7).

Paul had once worried about the effect his stern writing would have on them. He now rejoiced because the letter had moved them to a godly sorrow that caused them to repent. Instead of causing damage, good had been done. Sorrow that comes out of faith in God and desire to please him will cause the sorrowful to desire to change. Such sorrow will bring happiness because the result is the salvation of the one made sorry. A sorrow based on worldly considerations, such as sorrow for being caught or the bad effect on one's reputation, may bring a correction yet still result in eternal damnation (2 Cor. 7:8-10).

The case of the Corinthians is a good example of the good effects of godly sorrow. This sorrow caused them to quit being indifferent about their state and start showing concern. They wanted to wipe the sin away and make restitution. It upset them that they had been so lax in their attitude toward discipline. Although they feared that Paul would come with a rod to punish them, they still longed for his coming so that the matter might be settled and brought to a good conclusion. It caused them to get busy and punish the offenders so that the wrong might be righted. They showed their pure desire by completely caring for the matter as Paul, by inspiration, had instructed (2 Cor. 7:11).

DOING WHAT IS RIGHT IN THE SIGHT OF GOD

Paul's goal in writing to the Corinthians was not to straighten out a problem between two individuals, though the incestuous man was wrong and he had wronged his father. The greater cause for the letter was to see that they followed an inspired apostle's instruction and did what was right in God's sight. Because they received Paul's message and turned back to God, Paul was comforted. Paul had further joy in that Titus, who may have had misgivings about delivering the letter, had not been depressed but uplifted by their response. Paul had eased these misgivings by telling Titus that the gospel would be well received by the Corinthians.

It is interesting to note the apostle had had no time of loosening or relaxing before Titus' return (2:13; 7:5). Their actions had verified the truthfulness of his assurances concerning their loyalty and prevented both him and them being shamed by a negative response (2 Cor. 7:12-14).

Several good things resulted from the Corinthians' response to the first letter. Above all, they had dealt with the sin in the church. Titus' love for the Corinthians grew because of their fearful response to the message of truth delivered. Additionally, Paul's confidence in them was strengthened, and he was assured that they would strive to do what was right in God's eyes (2 Cor. 7:15-16).

REFLECTION & DISCUSSION

1. In what ways did Paul act like a loving father in his relationship with the church in Corinth?

2. What things did Titus report to Paul concerning the Corinthian church's view of the apostle?

3. What impact did godly sorrow have on the lives of the Corinthian Christians?

4. What goals did Paul have in writing his first letter to Corinth?

5. What lessons can we learn from the response of the Corinthian church to Paul's first letter?

8

COMPLETING A COMMITMENT

2 CORINTHIANS 8:1-24

THE GIFT FROM MACEDONIA

Paul gave instructions concerning a collection in 1 Cor. 16:1-3. He now wrote to inform the Corinthian brethren about the grace God had shown the brethren in Macedonia, which would include Philippi, Berea, and Thessalonica. "Grace" is the opportunity to do good for others, for which Christians should be thankful. The money was a blessing from God given to aid poor saints at Jerusalem (2 Cor. 8:1).

The gift was remarkable because, as McGarvey and Pendleton state, Macedonia had just been through three civil wars (210). The people were impoverished to the point that their taxes had been lightened. The church was made even poorer by persecution (2 Thess. 1:4). They were put to the test by their affliction and poverty. They coupled this, however, with their joy at receiving the gospel and gave abundantly, especially given their poverty (2 Cor. 8:2).

Before Paul had a chance to ask for a contribution, these people gave over and above their means. They then begged Paul to deliver the money to those in need in Jerusalem. They gave so freely because they first gave themselves over totally to God. Their service was then given to the apostles as God's servants. The reason their gift exceeded all Paul's hopes is evidently the fact that they counted all they had as God's (2 Cor. 8:3-5).

COMPLETING A COMMITMENT

The apostle was encouraged by the Macedonian response and sent Titus back to finish the collection at Corinth. Paul used the Macedonian example to encourage, not promote, competition. The Corinthian brethren, after all, possessed many of the gifts of the Spirit and Christian virtues. Their father in the faith now encouraged them to add one more good work (2 Cor. 8:6-7).

Giving must be a personal decision to be of any value to the giver, so Paul was not commanding them to give. Instead, he intended to use an example to inspire them. The gift would be a clear measure of their love. It was impossible for Paul to speak of a gift as the measure of one's love without thinking of Jesus' great sacrifice. He gave up heaven and its riches to come to earth and die for us (2 Cor. 8:8-9; Phil. 1:4-8; Heb. 2:9).

One's giving must be willingly done (2 Cor. 9:7), so the apostle would not command them to give. He did encourage them to finish the work they had started. They had promised to do this work, and he was pleading with them to keep their promise. The Father will accept a gift that is given willingly and freely. The greatness of the gift is not determined by the amount, but by amount coupled with ability. The best example of this is the widow and her gift of two mites (2 Cor. 8:10-12; Mark 12:41-44).

PROVIDING FOR BASIC NEEDS

Paul's purpose was not to make the Corinthians poor so that those in Jerusalem might be made richer. He wanted them to give out of their overflow that others might have their basic needs provided. At some time in the future, the Corinthians might have needs that could be met by someone else's abundance (2 Cor. 8:13-14).

No one in the wilderness had any usable manna leftover, and no one lacked for a good amount to consume (2 Cor. 8:15; Exod. 16:17-18). McGarvey and Pendleton write, "Now that which God effected by irresistible law under the old dispensation, he was now seeking to effect under the new dispensation through the gracious influence of brotherly love. Our differences in ability make it inevitable that some shall surpass others in the gathering of wealth; but as selfishness gives place to Christian love, the inequality of earthly possessions will become more even" (213).

THANKFULNESS FOR BRETHREN

Paul thanked God that he had caused Titus to have the same loving concern for the Corinthians' spiritual growth as Paul had. Titus not only was willing to go back and encourage them to take up a collection, but he had also prepared to go before being asked (2 Cor. 8:16-17).

Another brother, who was widely praised for his work on behalf of the gospel, went with Titus. This second brother could be trusted because of the above-mentioned praise and because he had been appointed to help Paul carry the gift to Jerusalem (2 Cor. 8:18-19). Paul was glad to have companions so that he would be above suspicion in the handling of the money. He wanted to be right in God's eyes and have a good reputation among men if possible. Paul sent a third brother with them who had often been used by him and had proven a determined worker in God's service. This brother's determination had grown stronger because of his knowledge of the Corinthians' work (2 Cor. 8:20-22).

Paul noted that Titus was his partner in the work at Corinth, which was likely to stop all objections to the three. Further, the other two were men sent by churches to deliver messages. They had apparently proven faithful by delivering the whole message without any changes. These men had plainly given over their lives to Jesus with the sole purpose of glorifying the Savior, also. Since the messengers deserved their trust, Paul asked the Corinthians to show their love in the collection of the gift. He wanted them to show it because he knew they had it and had confidently affirmed to the messengers that they would display it.

REFLECTION & DISCUSSION

1. What things can we learn from the Macedonians' gift?

2. How did Paul praise people while calling them to action?

3. Discuss the lessons Paul delivered about giving.

4. What can we learn from the children of Israel and the manna?

5. What characteristics did Paul see in Titus and the unnamed brother that you would like others to see in you?

9

GIVING

2 CORINTHIANS 9:1-15

AVOIDING EMBARRASSMENT

The American Standard Version begins 2 Cor. 9 with, "For as touching the ministry," which indicates Paul is continuing a discussion. He knew that the Corinthians would give to care for the poor saints, so this writing was more than was necessary, or "superfluous" (Thompson 121). He believed them when, over a year before, they had committed themselves to give. He used their commitment as a means of moving others to action, much as he used the Macedonians to stimulate the Corinthians (2 Cor. 8:1-5). In fact, the example of Achaia had stirred Macedonia to its liberality (2 Cor. 9:1-2). Thompson says the word "majority" literally describes the "greatest number" (122).

Paul sent Titus and two other brethren (2 Cor. 8:16-22) to take up the collection so that his good words about the Corinthian readiness would not prove empty. The apostle did not want to be ashamed, to say nothing of the shame the Corinthians would feel if someone from Macedonia should come and find their example not as good as the Macedonians' own gift. Thus, the brethren were sent ahead of Paul so that the Corinthians could give freely rather than feeling pressured into giving because they feared Paul's rebuke. The only gift that has real value to a Christian is the one that is freely given (2 Cor. 9:3-5; Phil. 4:17).

THE CHEERFUL GIVER

It is obvious to farmers the world over that sparingly sowing seed will result in a sparse harvest. It is equally obvious that, with proper weather conditions and good timing, bountifully sowing seed will result in a plentiful harvest. The same law stands in the spiritual realm. Christians should give out of their heart's desire and not as others require. They should not give if such giving brings tears and sorrow as they part from their money. Morgan says the word "cheerful" might be rendered "hilarious," conveying the idea of "laughter, and song, and cheer" (254). We should want to laugh and sing for the joy of giving (2 Cor. 9:6-7).

God can favor his people with temporal good and will when they cheerfully give. The apostle used the word "all," or "every," five times in v. 8, ultimately letting Christians know there would be "an abundance," literally "enough," for every good work. Paul quoted Psa. 112:9 to show that the man who cheerfully gives will be provided for physically. It further shows that this man will always be able to give, since God will replenish his goods. The righteousness of the giver mentioned here describes general virtue or excellence as shown in giving to those in need (2 Cor. 9:8-9).

GIVING YIELDS BLESSINGS & THE GIVING OF THANKS

God causes the farmer to receive a harvest that provides for his needs and gives him seed to use the next time. The one who sows the seed of giving will see needs taken care of and seed, or money, provided for future giving. The freely given gift would multiply the giver's ability to give freely and cause the ones who received to glorify God. The word translated "service" describes the ceremonial service of a priest. The gift would then not only provide for the needs of the saints, but would also go up to God in the form of thanks given (2 Cor. 9:10-12).

Paul said that those in Jerusalem would give thanks for the provision of their needs and for the Corinthians. They would give praise to God for the good Christians at Corinth who were truly converted, as their actions showed. They would give thanks for the generous gift and the knowledge that the needy everywhere could rely on Corinth. The Jerusalem saints would, as a result, pray for God's blessings on the Corinthians and that they might meet face to face and fellowship their generous brethren.

Any extended discussion of giving serves to remind Christians of the greatest gift ever given. The apostle was moved to thank God for the great gift of Jesus that brought about fellowship between the needy saints of Judea and the Christians in the church of God at Corinth. God's gift of his Son was, to Paul, indescribable, which literally means "not to be told throughout" (Vincent 337). Lipscomb said, "Jesus is the manifestation of God's love to man, and his love for man inspires those who trust him to love and serve others." Shepherd added, "but it is the great divine gift, and not its fruits in the lives of men, however rich and various, that passes the power of words to characterize" (126).

REFLECTION & DISCUSSION

1. How can your example, and that of your local church, be used to stimulate others to good works?

2. In addition to giving us the ability to make a living, what ways does God bless us?

3. Discuss the particular blessings promised to the cheerful and generous giver.

4. How could the church's funds be used to multiply thanksgiving to God?

5. Discuss the most powerful example of giving ever shown to the world.

10

THE SPIRITUAL WAR & PAUL'S AUTHORITY

2 CORINTHIANS 10:1-18

A PLEA FOR THE CORINTHIAN CHRISTIANS TO CHANGE

The early chapters of 2 Corinthians largely address the part of the church loyal to Paul. The apostle now turns to deal with his accusers. He included Timothy in previous thoughts, often using the word "we" for he and Timothy. The change to the word "I" clearly shows he stands alone for his defense. The apostle pleaded with them in "the meekness and gentleness of Christ" (10:1). "'Meekness' is the quality in the heart, and its expression is 'gentleness' in dealing with poor sinners" (Lenski 1197-1198).

Those challenging Paul's apostleship apparently accused him of being weak while with them and bold in his writing when away from them. He wrote with a sharp tone in his letters and pleaded with them to change. He desired their actions to be such as to allow him to continue to be meek and gentle when they were face to face. He was not going to deal so gently with his accusers. He did not want to use the power God had given him to prove his own spirituality and disprove the false charges that he served only his fleshly desires (10:2).

SPIRITUAL WARFARE

Paul and his assistants did walk in the flesh and exhibit all the weaknesses pertaining thereto. He denied using human tactics, like slandering his enemies to destroy them or adjusting his speech to please others and satisfy personal desires. All of the apostle's power, and that of his assistants, was from God and was based upon God's Word (1 Cor. 4:19-21; 5:4). Like the cross, God's power might seem weak to the men of this world. However, it is fully capable of "pulling down, destruction, demolition" (Thayer 311) of "fortified places" (Thompson 137).

The purpose of Christianity is to throw out all human thinking and place God in complete control. Human reasoning "may be impressive philosophies, findings of science, or the arguments of the common man with which he tries to satisfy the little thinking he is able to do" (Lenski 1207). The Christian should subject every thought, which would formerly have been worldly, to God's uses and intents. Their obedience would only be complete when they punished those who were upsetting the unity of the church through their continual agitation. Paul planned to punish them when he came, but he paused to give all those who would obey a chance to submit fully to the will of God (10:3-6).

DEALING WITH DETRACTORS

The apostle's detractors were using a worldly standard of judgment when they looked at the outside to determine value. Such is a shallow measure. Paul was at least equal to those who opposed him (Acts 9:15; 15:25; Gal. 2:9). He knew that he could boast in his authority as opposed to theirs and that his boast would be backed up. He would not fall to his shame. However, God gave Paul that great power to build up the church, not tear it down as others with less power apparently would do (10:7-8).

Christ's apostle to the Gentiles could back his strong letters with power if it was necessary when he arrived. Some falsely accused him of being powerful in his writing but weak when present. He wanted them to know he would back his words with power and prompt action when he was present with them (10:9-11).

Paul did not see himself as an equal to his opponents in their ability to exaggerate their own power and authority. Apparently, they had accused him of commending himself (2 Cor. 3:1; 5:12), but they were describing their own problem. Within their own narrow circle, they looked big to themselves, but showed their lack of knowledge of the way things were elsewhere. Christians will be judged by Christ's Word (John 12:48), not their own consciences. Each should make Christ the standard of comparison instead of using the world as a measuring rod (10:12).

THE STANDARD OF MEASURING ONESELF

Paul did not measure himself by men. He measured himself by the area in which God had given him to work. His sphere of preaching was the area where Christ had not been named (Rom. 15:20), which included Corinth when he started the work there. He could confidently say that he did not go out of the sphere assigned to him when he preached at Corinth. Going to Corinth was actually a means of fulfilling his mission (10:13-14).

The apostle did not have to build on other men's labors to find work. He was forced to confine his labors to them until they grew. Their lack of growth kept him from furthering the gospel elsewhere. Paul intended to go on and establish churches in other lands needing the gospel when he finished at Corinth. He did not need to seize someone else's work as his opponents had done (10:15-16).

"He who glories, let him glory in the Lord" is a paraphrase of Jer. 9:23-24. Paul gave all the glory for his success to the Lord, unlike those challenging him. Self-approval and commendation carry no weight. God's approval is based on service actually rendered and carries lasting value (10:17-18).

REFLECTION & DISCUSSION

1. What is the difference between weakness and meekness as shown through gentleness?

2. What purpose do Christians have (cf. 2 Cor. 10:3-6)?

3. Using Paul and David as examples, discuss the importance of being strong within.

4. Why is it important to measure ourselves against Christ vs. men? What impact would one have over the other?

5. What was the source of Paul's success? To whom should we give the glory?

11

PAUL'S APOSTLESHIP & SUFFERING

2 CORINTHIANS 11:1-33

THE CORINTHIAN'S FAITHFULNESS, PAUL'S DESIRE

Paul did not see any point in the mindless bragging of those opposing him, but he asked the Corinthians to bear with him while he proved his apostleship. He further stated that he knew they would bear with him. His jealousy over them did not originate out of a selfish desire for gain. Instead, he only wanted them to be faithful to God. The apostle had arranged an engagement for the Corinthian church with Christ. This is reminiscent of Jesus' description of the bridegroom and his friend (John 3:29). The waiting time, before Christ came to claim her, gave her opportunity to prove her faithfulness and show she would not flirt with or love another (2 Cor. 11:1-2).

The apostle to the Gentiles was also worried that they would be drawn away from the truth by false teachers promising attractive rewards, as Satan had drawn away Eve. They had the pure truth and should spurn any other teaching. If the false teacher, who probably stands for all the false teachers, had presented another plan of salvation or savior, Paul might understand their hearing him out. These claimed to preach the same Savior and salvation, yet denied what the Lord had taught (2 Cor. 11:3-4).

PAUL'S SACRIFICE AS AN APOSTLE

It appears some in Corinth were claiming to be "super" apostles and that Paul, as the Lord's real apostle, feared they would tolerate false teaching. Paul said he was equal to all of them, which was demonstrated when James, Peter, and John gave him the right hand of fellowship (Gal. 2:9). He admitted that he was not a great orator, but he was great in knowledge and made it plain and understandable in his speaking. It was true that he had not accepted payment for his work among them, but that was so no one would be hindered from obeying the gospel. Ironically, some were saying he refused the pay of an apostle because he knew he was not one (1 Cor. 9:1-15). He simply asked if it was a sin for him to refuse pay (2 Cor. 11:5-7).

Others were deprived of their needs so that Paul might preach to the Corinthians without charge. He had gone without necessities, rather than lose his influence by accepting wages from the Corinthian church, even though it was well within his rights as a teacher of the gospel (Gal. 6:6; 1 Cor. 9:1-18). He waited until brethren came from Macedonia, saw his need, and cared for him, a likely reference to the incident reported in Phil. 4:15-16. Paul, while working in Achaia, intended to continue to refuse help from them and would continue to boast about it. Some wondered why he did this. They may have suggested that it was out of a lack of love. Paul called God as his witness that this was not true (2 Cor. 11:8-11).

Their father in the faith refused to give all of his reasons for spurning payment for his work while among them. He did not want to talk openly about their weakness, which was part of the reason. He did say that he would continue to refuse pay so the false teachers would continue to be exposed. They took pay from the Corinthians, while he did not. Those that accepted pay and opposed Paul were impostors pretending to be apostles. They worked, but hidden beneath their work were bad motives and intentions. Since they were not called of Christ, they could be described as self-made apostles (2 Cor. 11:12-13).

Satan often presents himself to man as one seeking man's good, as he did with Eve in the garden of Eden. It should come as no surprise that his ministers likewise portray themselves as great religious leaders seeking man's good. All who would turn God's people from the truth are ministers of Satan. They deceive and will be punished for such deception (2 Cor. 11:14-15; Rev. 21:8).

PAUL'S REASONS FOR GLORYING

Glorying had been the main subject. However, Paul had strayed from it twice since v. 1. Driven by his opponents to boast, Paul asked the readers' indulgence. Delivering the message of Christ does not require boasting, however, Paul did it to show he had more to glory in than the false teachers and could beat them on their own ground. The false teachers had boasted about fleshly things while downgrading Paul in the same, so he turned to show the weakness of their argument (2 Cor. 11:16-18).

The brethren in Corinth thought so highly of themselves that they patiently listened to foolish boasters. They had been patient with the false teachers while they placed themselves in bondage to false authority and doctrine. They had paid the high wage demands. They had even stooped to the position of slaves who must suffer the great insult of being slapped. Paul, in contrast, had spoken to them in *meek*ness while in Corinth, which had been misunderstood to be *weak*ness. He was determined to show the boasters his superiority, knowing it would be wasted, since Christ had called him to be an apostle and would judge him (2 Cor. 11:19-21).

There can be no doubt that the false teachers were Judaizers. Paul was their equal in that religion, despite their apparent claims to the contrary (Acts 22:2-3; Phil. 3:5). He was also their superior in following Christ. They might have said he was mad for making such a statement, and he admitted that making such an argument was insane. They had lived off another man's labors (2 Cor. 10:15-16), but he excelled in real labor. He listed his suffering, not accomplishments, as proof of his service to the Lord (2 Cor. 11:22-23).

He had endured thirty-nine stripes from the Jews on five different occasions. The Law allowed forty (Deut. 25:3), but the Jews left one off to avoid breaking the Law by accidental miscount. Three times Paul was beaten with rods, which was Roman scourging (Acts 16:22-24). He was stoned once, which was usually a Jewish punishment for blasphemy (Acts 14:19). The dangerous travel of that era had likewise resulted in the apostle being shipwrecked three times, even spending a night and a day in the sea. Paul used the word "perils," or "dangerous encounters," six times in v. 26. These included troubles with the Gentiles who were enraged because he turned some away from idols and false brethren who apparently sought to ruin him, as in Corinth. He worked till work was painful and lost sleep to help others (2 Cor. 11:24-27).

In addition to the physical suffering he endured, Paul also worried about the churches and wrongs he was called upon to right within them. He was concerned about every Christian that faced hard times. He felt their weaknesses and burned with anger when someone acted in a way that led to a Christian being caught in the devil's trap (2 Cor. 11:28-29).

The apostle to the Gentiles, when forced to boast, would not tell of his great accomplishments. Rather, he put his enemies to shame by showing the suffering he endured for the cross. Any doubt concerning the truthfulness of Paul's statements about his weakness should have been laid aside as he made a great call for God to be his witness. His problems in Damascus were related by Luke in Acts 9:23-25. He had escaped from wicked hands when the gates were closed. The brethren had assisted him in leaving by lowering him from a window in a house along the wall (2 Cor. 11:30-33).

REFLECTION & DISCUSSION

1. What thoughts arise when you think of the church being engaged to Christ?

2. What lessons can we learn from Paul's means of support while in Corinth?

3. Today, in what ways does Satan present himself as one seeking our good?

4. From the book of Acts, list some of the things Paul may have been describing when he spoke of suffering he endured.

5. How can we show concern for all the churches like Paul did?

12

A VISION, A THORN, & LOVE

2 CORINTHIANS 12:1-21

A VISION

Paul continued boasting (12:1, 5, 6, 9) because of the false teachers, though such would ordinarily be undesirable. The visions of which he spoke would have been given by God, while revelations were used to expose truths God had not shown before. The specific vision to which the apostle referred involved a man, which was Paul according to v. 7, caught up into the third heaven. The birds fly in the first heaven, stars shine in the second, and God abides in the third. Paul could not tell whether he went bodily or only in spirit. Some think the passing of fourteen years would place Paul back in Antioch (Acts 13:1-3). It seems more likely that he was speaking of the stoning at Lystra (Acts 14:19-20). This would explain why he could not say whether he was in or out of the body (2 Cor. 12:1-3).

Jewish writers often used parallelism, a technique wherein one writes of a matter twice using slightly different but synonymous words so the reader is sure to understand. Paradise, as used in this verse, apparently refers to the "third heaven." Paradise is used in the

Septuagint in Gen. 2:8 and Ezek. 31:8. It is also included in Luke 23:43; Rev. 2:7; 22:2. The purpose of Paul's vision is unknown, though it must have helped him face the trials already mentioned. It is clear that God would not allow him to talk about it (2 Cor. 12:4).

Such a man had certainly been honored, and Paul could boast about the man's honor. He, when speaking directly of himself, would only glory in his weakness. Boasting was foolish if one exaggerated his ability. Paul could boast without that, but he chose to stand on his speech and actions. He did not want men to honor him for the blessings God had given him (2 Cor. 12:5-6).

A REQUEST, A REFUSAL, & A REALIZATION

Paul could have been destroyed by pride because of what God had shown him. So he was given a "thorn," or "pointed piece of wood," in the flesh that kept him from becoming overly proud. This physical condition kept him from being puffed up because of the spiritual revelations he had received. Paul prayed that God would cause the thorn to depart. This prayer, like the one Jesus offered in the Garden of Gethsemane, was heard, but answered in the negative (2 Cor. 12:7-8).

The Father made it clear that his power is most fully recognized when men are weakest. Men of faith, like Gideon, learned that God does not need the things men would consider necessary to show power to achieve his ends. Paul, therefore, boasted of his weakness, because that was the time God's power would be the strongest in his life (2 Cor. 12:9).

Lipscomb and Shepherd say "injuries" refer to "the wrong springing from violence, injury, affront, and insult, to which there are frequent allusions in this epistle" (161). They went on to reference 1:17; 3:1; 7:8; 10:10; 11:6, 8, 16. The spiritual man's hours of greatest weakness are the times God's greatest strength is brought to bear on his behalf (2 Cor. 12:10).

THE SIGNS OF AN APOSTLE

The Corinthian Christians' failure to defend Paul forced him into boasting. The apostle knew that he was nothing without God. Even at that, he was greater than the false teachers who set themselves up as the chiefest of apostles. There had been an apostle among them, but it was Paul. He was supported in his claim by the signs Christ had promised (Mark 16:17-18). These same words were used by Peter about the events of Pentecost (Acts 2:22). Paul also told the Thessalonians that the "wicked" one would deceive them with things like these (2 Thess. 2:9). The church at Corinth had, in reality, the same blessings and gifts as any church started by an apostle. The only thing they lacked was a demand of high wages by Paul, like the false apostles had made (2 Cor. 12:11-13).

PAUL'S LOVE FOR THE CHURCH IN CORINTH

Paul loved the Corinthian Christians like parents love their children, so he would again refuse pay during his coming visit (1 Cor. 4:14-15). He did not seek their money, but the salvation of their souls. He would give up all he had for the salvation of his spiritual children, just as a physical father would give up all he had for the physical needs of his children. Paul wondered if that greater love would cause them to love him less. He was, nonetheless, willing for their love to be lessened if they could benefit. His accusers, naturally, claimed he was using such tactics to trick them into paying him (2 Cor. 12:14-16).

The apostle had taken no money personally, so they apparently accused him of using Titus, his messenger, and others to take the money through a false collection. Paul asked if Titus received wages from them or took up the collection personally. All the money that had been given had, instead, been kept in the church treasury (1 Cor. 16:1-2). Paul was laying the facts out before God, who is the judge, instead of defending himself before them. He had done everything to teach them, as God knew (2 Cor. 12:17-19).

The apostle, their father in the faith, had worked with them and written to them so they would put away sin. He hoped he would not find them still in it when he arrived. If they were in sin, which he did not want, he would discipline them, which they did not want. He specifically did not want to find them having "contentions," which was a clear sign of spiritual immaturity and had been present in Corinth before the apostle's first letter (1 Cor. 1:11). Nor did he want to find them in the midst of jealousies, described by Thayer as "an envious and contentious rivalry" (271), or "tumults," which are "disturbances, disorders" (21). Paul did not want to find such evil since he would be humiliated and forced to weep over those who refused to turn from their evil ways. Repentance would cause them to change their minds and ways. They should no longer be divided into factions that resulted in them sinfully attacking one another (2 Cor. 12:20-21).

REFLECTION & DISCUSSION

1. What can we learn from Paul's description of the third heaven?

2. How did Paul describe God's refusal to take away the thorn in the flesh?

3. What are the signs of an apostle?

4. How can a Christian show motherly love for fellow Christians?

5. How can we help one another avoid, or come out of, sin?

13

PAUL'S TRIP & CLOSING THOUGHTS

2 CORINTHIANS 13:1-14

PAUL'S TRIP & DEALING WITH FALSE TEACHERS

Paul had visited Corinth twice before and was now prepared to make a third trip. He was prepared to deal further with the false teachers, if necessary. His actions would not be rash, but would be confirmed by two or three witnesses (Num. 35:30; Deut. 17:6; 19:15; Matt. 18:15-17). The time for patiently waiting had passed and any still involved in sin would be punished severely. Division and carnal thinking must end (2 Cor. 13:1-2).

They had challenged Paul's inspiration and accused him of preaching a weak Christ. He responded by reminding them that Christ's power had been evident in his work in Corinth. It was true that Christ was crucified because of weakness, but that was man's weakness. It was also true that he was raised from the dead in power, God's power (Rom. 4:24; 6:4; 8:11; 1 Pet. 1:21). The apostle, because of Christ, had suffered trials and the weaknesses of man. He was now prepared to show God's power to them in punishment (2 Cor. 13:3-4).

PASSING THE TEST & PREFERRED GENTLENESS

Paul challenged his readers to test themselves as Christians, just as they had tested him as an apostle. Jesus would be in them if they were obedient (John 14:23). Those who failed the test would be reprobates (Jer. 6:27-30), that is "tested and found false, spurious, either not believing the real gospel but something else or only pretending to believe the gospel while not really believing it" (Lenski 1333). The apostle hoped they knew that he would not fail the test (2 Cor. 13:5-6).

His prayer for the Corinthians was that they be faithful. He did not pray this so that his name would be cleared and they would again respect him. Rather, he would allow his name to remain stained in their sight if they could be found faithful. He did not rejoice over a chance to show his power because of the evil in the church at Corinth. Paul was, in fact, praying that the good in the lives of Corinthian Christians would cause his authority to go without proof. Their father in the faith would gladly have had them keep on thinking of him as weak and without authority, since that would mean he had not been required to discipline them.

Paul prayed that they might be made "complete," which is a word describing the setting of a broken bone. His desire was that they would change while he was away from them. All his authority and power were intended to be used to make congregations grow. He hated the thought of using that power to cut out infected and diseased members (2 Cor. 13:7-10).

THOUGHTS IN CLOSING

Paul wrapped his letter up using a word, translated "farewell," which can mean "rejoice" according to the margin of the American Standard Version. The apostle called them "brethren" to show that the letter was written in a spirit of love. He urged them: "let yourselves 'be completely fitted out, let yourselves be admonished'" (Lenski 1338). We might say they should let themselves be changed by the comforting correction the apostle had given in this epistle, which would lead to them being perfected in the sight of God. They would be of the same mind if they all submitted to the rule of God's Word in their teaching and general demeanor. Such submission would bring peace. Being more concerned with the good of others vs. self would result in peace and love (2 Cor. 13:11).

They were urged to greet each other as friends and brethren. Those who were with Paul sent their greetings to them as brethren. It is interesting that Paul's prayer for them began with his desire for them to have the grace of the Lord Jesus Christ. The apostle to the Gentiles had already told them that Jesus had given up the riches of heaven to come to earth and live as a humble servant so that men could know the riches of salvation (8:9; Rom. 5:8). Christ's followers go to the throne of grace to find help when they are in need (Heb. 4:16). "The love of God referred to is the love with which God embraces his own and not the love that reaches out to make men his own. God's love can bestow thousands of gifts upon believers that he could not possibly bestow upon people who are not yet believers or who are unbelievers" (Lenski 1339). God's people, blessed with the grace of their Lord and love of the Father, naturally enjoy fellowship, or communion, with the Holy Spirit (2 Cor. 13:11-14).

REFLECTION & DISCUSSION

1. What lessons might we learn from Paul's handling of the trouble with the false teachers?

2. In what ways can we test ourselves to be assured we are in the faith?

3. Discuss Paul's desire for the church. What was he willing to give up if it could be achieved?

4. What words can we use to make our true love for fellow Christians stand out.

5. Discuss Paul's prayer for the church in Corinth. What types of things should we include in our prayers for our brethren?

PERSONAL NOTES

PERSONAL NOTES

PERSONAL NOTES

PERSONAL NOTES

PERSONAL NOTES

PERSONAL NOTES

PERSONAL NOTES

PERSONAL NOTES

PERSONAL NOTES

PERSONAL NOTES

PERSONAL NOTES

PERSONAL NOTES

PERSONAL NOTES

BIBLIOGRAPHY

Barnes, Albert. *II Corinthians and Galatians*. Grand Rapids, MI: Baker Book House, 1980. Print. Notes on the New Testament Explanatory and Practical.

Lenski, R. C. H. *The Interpretation of St. Paul's First and Second Epistle to the Corinthians*. Columbus, OH: Wartburg, 1946. Print.

Lipscomb, David, and J. W. Shepherd. *Second Corinthians and Galatians*. Vol. III. Nashville: Gospel Advocate, 1976. Print. A Commentary on the New Testament Epistles.

McGarvey, J. W., and Philip Y. Pendleton. *Thessalonians, Corinthians, Galatians and Romans*. Delight, AR: Gospel Light, N.d. Print.

Morgan, G. Campbell. *The Corinthian Letters of Paul: An Exposition of I and II Corinthians*. Old Tappan, NJ: Fleming H. Revell, 1946. Print.

Thayer, Joseph H. *A Greek-English Lexicon of the New Testament*. Grand Rapids: Baker Book House, 1977. Print.

Thompson, James. *The Second Letter of Paul to the Corinthians*. Ed. Everett Ferguson. Austin, TX: R. B. Sweet, 1970. Print. The Living Word Commentary.

Vincent, Marvin R. *Word Studies in the New Testament: The Epistles of Paul*. Vol. III. Grand Rapids, MI: Wm. B. Eerdmans, 1965. Print.

www.ingramcontent.com/pod-product-compliance
Lightning Source LLC
Chambersburg PA
CBHW060534030426
42337CB00021B/4249